Lila and Andy learn about

Artificial Intelligence

Discover Large Language Models and Prompt Engineering

Kenneth Adams

Book Cover by Kenneth Adams
Illustrations by Kenneth Adams
First Edition 2025

ISBN: 978-1-998552-20-7

Important Note for Parents and Guardians

This book introduces children to artificial intelligence and how to communicate with AI tools. While interacting with AI can be educational and fun, adult supervision is recommended, especially for younger children.

When children use AI tools:

- <u>Supervise their access.</u> Many AI platforms have age restrictions (typically 13+) due to data privacy concerns.
- <u>Protect their privacy.</u> Teach children never to share personal information with AI systems.
- <u>Monitor content.</u> While AI tools have safety measures, they can occasionally generate inappropriate content if prompted in certain ways.
- <u>Encourage critical thinking.</u> Remind them AI can make mistakes or present incorrect information. Encourage them to verify important facts from reliable sources.
- <u>Set healthy boundaries.</u> Balance AI interaction with other activities and human interaction.

The exercises in this book teach valuable skills for responsible AI interaction. Your involvement helps children develop digital literacy while staying safe.

Hi, I'm Lila, and this is my brother Andy. I'm the one who's always got my nose in a book, exploring different fictional worlds, and Andy's usually trying to beat the next level of his favorite online game.

We may have different hobbies, but we're both curious about how things work. That's why we got excited about <u>Artificial Intelligence</u>, or <u>AI</u>, and that's what we're here to tell you about!

Today, we'll explore an amazing concept called a Large Language Model and how to talk to it using prompts.

Ready to learn? Let's go!

What are Large Language Models?

Have you ever heard about AI assistants like ChatGPT, Claude, or Gemini? People often wonder if they're robots. Well, they're definitely not robots.

<u>Large Language Models</u>, or <u>LLMs</u> for short, are a specific type of AI. These LLMs are really smart computer programs that understand human language. In fact, they understand it so well that they can create their own conversations.

When scientists create an LLM, they feed it enormous amounts of text using very powerful computers. The information comes from millions of books, newspaper articles, websites, and other written materials. Imagine someone who has read almost every book ever written, more than anyone could read in a thousand lifetimes! That's what these LLMs are like.

Did you know the "Large" in Large Language Model refers to the huge amount of data and computing power needed to create these AI systems? Some are trained on more text than a person could read in their entire lifetime!

Did you know Large Language Models look at words in groups called "tokens?" Sometimes a token is a whole word, and sometimes just part of a word.

Once the information is loaded, the LLM studies all these documents and learns to spot patterns in the text. They figure out which words often go together, how sentences are formed, and which ideas belong with each other. The more information they study, the better they get at recognizing the way humans write and talk.

But here's the interesting part. LLMs don't truly "understand" like people do. While these language models recognize word patterns extremely well, they don't have experiences like ours. They've never enjoyed hearing the school bell ring on the last day before summer holiday. They've never craved a burger and fries or played outside in the rain. Their conversations come from making smart guesses about what words should come next in a sentence.

While LLMs know what words usually go together, they don't really know what the words mean. An LLM can write a beautiful paragraph about how ice cream tastes without ever having tasted it themselves! That's because they're not alive. LLMs don't have senses like smell, touch, or taste.

How do Large Language Models Work?

Let's explore how LLMs work. How do these AI models know what to say?

Here's a simple way to understand it. Let's think of an easy sentence and try to fill in the blank.

"The bird sits on the _____."

What do you think the bird sits on? A "roof," "fence," or "branch," perhaps? And you'd be right! It could be any of those. By guessing what word comes next, you're doing exactly what an LLM does.

You've probably read or heard lots of sentences like that, so your brain recognizes patterns of words. You can make good guesses about what word might fit. An LLM works the same way, just on a much bigger scale. When you give an LLM some text, it guesses what comes next, one word at a time.

But here's the amazing part. LLMs don't just guess one word. They build entire sentences, paragraphs, and even full stories this way!

Let's try another example.

"Today's math homework is about fractions and _____."

You might think of words like "percentages" or "decimals," but you probably wouldn't say "giraffes" or "basements," right? That's because those words don't usually show up in math homework. LLMs are smart enough to know the difference, even though they do not understand math like we do. They've read billions of sentences and studied these examples so well that they've learned that words like "fractions," "decimals," and "percentages" often appear near each other and usually fit together.

Imagine asking an LLM to write a short story about a kid who trains a friendly dragon. We've all heard that story before, right? The LLM has also seen many separate stories with children, dragons, and adventures, so it can mix those ideas together to create something brand new. It's not copying a specific story. Instead, it's reusing pieces it learned about to build something that feels fresh and original.

This is what makes LLMs so cool. They combine words and ideas in ways that make sense, even though they don't truly understand what they're saying. They have remembered billions of examples and can fit the pieces together like a giant puzzle made of words.

The Art of Prompt Engineering

Working with AI powered by LLMs is cool, but it's super important to learn how to talk to them.

We talk to these language models by giving them instructions, and we call these instructions <u>prompts</u>. When you prompt your friend to tell you a secret, you are asking them to do something specific. With AI, you are prompting it to do a task, like write a story or answer a question.

To make sure the AI does the best job it can, your instructions have to be very clear. This special skill of writing really good instructions or prompts is called <u>prompt engineering</u>.

Think of it like ordering a drink at your favorite coffee shop. If you just ask for "a drink," you could get anything! But if you ask for a 20-ounce iced, skinny, hazelnut macchiato with sugar-free syrup, a double shot of espresso, light ice, not no ice, and no whipped cream, the person making it knows exactly what you want.

AI powered by LLMs works the same way. When you tell the AI exactly what you want in your prompt, with lots of details, the answer or story you get back will be much more like what you were hoping for.

These images were generated using AI. When the prompt used to create the image becomes more detailed, the results become more impressive.

Prompt 1: A cartoon style treehouse.

Prompt 2: A cartoon style treehouse in a whimsical forest.

Prompt 3: A magical cartoon style treehouse with a winding staircase and glowing windows, nestled in a whimsical forest filled with giant mushrooms and fireflies, bathed in soft, ethereal light.

Prompt 1

Prompt 3

Prompt 2

So, when you chat with AI, be very clear about what you want. You can ask directly, like "Tell me about the Northern Lights." If you need the answer in a certain way, tell the AI to "Make a list" or "Write a short paragraph."

Mention who it's for with something simple like "Write it for someone my age." You can also share what you do or don't want to see, such as "Tell me a happy story with no sad parts!" And if size matters, just let the AI know how long or short you'd like the answer to be.

By being clear and providing detailed prompts, you can help the AI better understand what you want, to give you the best possible response!

Prompting Like a Pro

Now that you know the basics, here are more ways to sharpen your prompts.

Be Specific: You should be very specific about what you want. If you need to write a short story for a creative writing assignment, ask for specific elements to help you write an original story instead of asking the AI to write the whole story.

For example: "I want to write a story about a family going on an African holiday adventure. Can you give me five interesting safari settings I could use, and three possible adventures the family might go on? Also, suggest some wild animals that could appear in the story."

This way, you still get to be creative but have some great ideas to work with.

Just like our teachers give clear instructions, examples, and guidance to help us understand what we're learning at school, like how to speak correctly or do math, we must teach Artificial Intelligence by using clear, detailed prompts to get the best answers from it.

Give Examples: If you want the AI to write something in a particular style, give it an example of that style. Sometimes it is better to show than to explain. For example, if you want a poem that rhymes, include an example of a rhyming poem in your prompt.

Assign a Role: Asking the AI to pretend to be someone may produce a more useful response. For example, if you want to ask how to prevent wildfires, ask the AI to imagine it is a firefighter.

Break It Down: For more complicated questions or tasks, ask the AI to do it in steps: step one first, then step two, and so on.

Think About It: Ask the AI to think about the best way to answer your question. This will make the AI think more deeply about how to react to your prompt.

Share Background: Include helpful details, like "We are planning a surprise party for my Granny's eightieth birthday. What kinds of games were popular when she was my age?"

<u>What To Avoid:</u> You can tell the AI what you don't want to see in the answer. If you're doing a school project on bats, you can ask the AI to leave out scary facts about bats.

<u>Ask for Clarification:</u> To make sure the AI understands your prompt, end your prompt with "If you don't understand what I mean, ask me to explain."

<u>Try Again:</u> Remember that your first prompt may not always get you what you want. If the AI's answer is not quite what you were looking for, try again by changing your prompt to ask in a slightly different way. This cool technique, called iterative prompting, allows the AI to adjust its response to be just right for you. It's like telling a friend, "I don't get it," and they try to explain it again using different words.

To help you remember all these tips, there are five simple steps you can take to make your questions or prompts clear and helpful. It's called the C.R.A.F.T. Method, and while there are many different ways to structure a good prompt, we found this one helps us get better answers when talking to AI.

C is for Context: Give the AI background information about your work and ask your question clearly. For example, you might say, "I'm writing a school report about penguins, and I need to explain how they stay warm in Antarctica."

R is for Role: Tell the AI what job or character to play. You might say "act like a science teacher" or "pretend you're a friendly librarian who knows everything about penguins."

A is for Action: Explain exactly what you want the AI to do. Instead of just asking about penguins, say, "Write three short paragraphs explaining how penguins survive in the winter."

F is for Format: Tell the AI how to organize the answer. You might want a list, a story, bullet points, or information organized with chapters and headings.

T is for Tone and Target Audience: Tell the AI who will be reading or hearing the answer and how it should feel. You might say, "Explain this to middle schoolers in a fun, exciting way" or "Write this for adults, but keep it friendly and engaging."

Using C.R.A.F.T. helps the AI give you the best answers, which is exactly what you want when talking to AI.

Did you know, Artificial Intelligence can be confused, just like people? They're very smart in some ways, but they need humans to help guide them and check their work.

Finally, remember that AI systems like LLMs can make mistakes. Sometimes it might give an unfair or one-sided answer because it learned from things people wrote, which can be biased. Imagine it telling you 2 + 2 = 5. That's why it's always important to check the facts, especially for school assignments.

How to Use AI Responsibly

Artificial Intelligence, including Large Language Models, is pretty amazing, but it needs to be used the right way.

It might be tempting to ask AI to write your entire homework assignment for you, but that wouldn't help you in the long run. AI is meant to help us learn and be more creative, not to do our thinking for us. It is meant to be used as tools that make our lives easier. We shouldn't use it to do all the work for us.

It's like using a calculator to help us solve a math problem faster. The calculator can help with all the calculations we need to do, but we still need to know which operations to use to solve the problem. The calculator doesn't decide which numbers matter or how to use them. We do.

Here are some responsible ways to use AI.

Instead of asking it to write your whole assignment, you could ask it to explain parts of the assignment you don't understand, help you outline your ideas, or check your work after you've done it yourself.

You can ask the AI to create practice questions about something you're learning in school. Try answering them yourself first before checking if you got them right. This is a great way to see what you know and what you might need to study more.

When working on a history project, ask the AI to answer your questions by pretending it's a famous person from that time. This can give you ideas for your project without making the AI do the project for you.

When doing homework, ask AI to explain the things you don't understand, or to check your work for accuracy.

Create quiz sheets or mock exams with AI, and use them to test your knowledge.

Ask AI to pretend to be someone from the past, then ask them questions about that time.

Did you know the word "prompt" means to encourage someone to take action? When we prompt an AI, we're encouraging it to give us the kind of information or help we need!

Use AI to generate fresh ideas when you need inspiration.

When working with AI, staying safe online is very important

If you get stuck on a creative story or art project, ask the AI for one random idea or one interesting object to include. This can help spark your imagination when you feel you have no more good ideas.

After you write something yourself, you can ask the AI what parts of your work could use more details or examples. This way, you still do all the writing but get helpful tips on making it better.

When you read something confusing for a school assignment, ask the AI to explain it in simpler words. Once you understand it better, you can write about it using your own words and ideas.

Also, be careful with your private information. Just like when you use the internet, protecting your personal information when using AI tools is super important. Never share personal details like your home address, full name, phone number, or when exactly your family will be away on vacation. Some AI systems learn from what you tell them, meaning your information could be shared with others.

Now that we understand how to use AI tools responsibly, let's think about what these tools might mean for the future.

There are so many cool ways that AI, including LLMs, is being used to help with art, music, and science. It's amazing how quickly this technology is developing.

You might wonder if AI will take over jobs that people do. It's a good question, and one that many people are thinking about. AI will definitely change many jobs, as AI might take over some tasks in the future. But from what we've learned so far, AI works best when it works together with humans rather than replacing them.

It's kind of like when personal computers were first invented. Many people thought then that they would replace jobs. Instead, they took over some routine tasks, giving people time to focus on more interesting problems.

Knowing how to work with AI will be an important skill for kids our age, so learning about prompt engineering now is really valuable. Talking to AI properly isn't just about getting better homework help. It's about preparing for the future when these tools will be part of many different types of jobs.

Kids learning to talk to AI clearly will have a head start. They'll be able to use these tools to enhance their own creativity and problem-solving.

Now that you know more about AI, particularly Large Language Models (LLMs) and Prompt Engineering, try using these tools yourself by writing your own prompts.

Remember, talking to AI is a skill. Its usefulness will depend on how well you use it. AI is an incredible tool, but it works best when used to help with creativity and learning, not as a replacement for using your own amazing brain!

We hope you've enjoyed learning about this exciting technology with us. The world of AI is always changing and growing, and now you're ready to be part of it.

Who knows? Maybe someday you'll help create the next generation of AI systems that are even more helpful to people all over the world.

AI
Glossary

A glossary is like a mini-dictionary of terms with definitions.

Here's a glossary of terms associated with Artificial Intelligence.

AI (Artificial Intelligence) - Computers that can do smart things like humans, like understanding words, seeing pictures, or making decisions in a game.

AGI (Artificial General Intelligence) - Imagine a future computer brain that could learn anything a human can, maybe even better! Like a super-smart robot from the movies that can do all kinds of different things. Scientists are still working on this - we don't have true AGI yet!

Algorithm - Think of this like a step-by-step recipe that a computer follows. Just like you follow steps to make cookies, computers follow algorithms to solve problems.

Alignment - Making sure AI systems do what humans want them to do and follow our values. It's like teaching a helper robot to be helpful in the way we actually want, not in ways that might accidentally cause problems.

Anthropomorphism - This is when we pretend computers or robots have feelings like people do. Remember, even though AI can seem smart, it doesn't have real feelings or thoughts like you do!

API (Application Programming Interface) - This is like a special messenger that helps different computer programs talk to each other. Like how you might use a translator when talking to someone who speaks a different language.

Attention Mechanism - This is how AI learns to focus on important stuff. Just like how you pay attention to the most important parts when reading a story, AI learns which parts of information matter most.

Bias - When an AI is unfair because it learned from unfair information. For example, if it only ever saw pictures of dogs as pets, it might think cats can't be pets, too!

Bot - A simple computer program that does the same job over and over without getting tired or bored. Like a robot vacuum that cleans your floor all by itself.

Chain-of-Thought (CoT) Prompting - Asking the AI to show its work, like when your teacher asks you to show how you solved a math problem, not just give the answer.

Chatbot - A computer program you can have a conversation with by typing messages, like texting a friend, but it's a computer!

ChatGPT - A famous LLM (Large Language Model) from OpenAI that's really good at writing stories, answering questions, and having conversations using words.

Claude - Another powerful LLM, like ChatGPT, built by Anthropic to be extra helpful, honest, and safe when talking with people.

Context - The background information that helps you understand what something means. For AI, it's like remembering what you were just talking about, so it knows what you mean now.

Context window - How much stuff the AI can remember at once during your conversation. Modern LLMs can remember much more than earlier ones - from thousands to millions of words! It's like how some friends can remember your entire story while others might forget parts.

Conversational AI - Computer programs that are designed to have normal back-and-forth talks with people, just like you might chat with a friend.

Data - Information that computers use to learn, like pictures, words, or sounds. It's like the food that helps AI grow smarter!

Deep learning - Teaching computers using fake "brains" with many layers that help them learn really complicated stuff, kind of like how you learn more complex things as you grow up.

Embeddings - A way computers turn words into special number codes, like a secret language that helps them understand how words are related to each other.

Ethical AI - Making sure we build and use AI in ways that are fair and good for everyone. It's like having good playground rules so everyone can have fun safely.

Feedback - Telling the AI how it did, if its answer was good or wrong, so it can learn to do better next time, like when a teacher marks your homework.

Few-shot prompting - Showing the AI a couple of examples of what you want, like showing a new student a couple of ways to solve a math problem before asking them to solve one.

Fine-tuning - Taking an AI that already knows lots of stuff and giving it extra practice on one specific thing. Like a soccer player who already knows the game but practices extra on penalty kicks.

Generative AI - AI that can create new stuff, like writing a story, drawing a picture, or making music that didn't exist before!

Gemini - A family of multimodal AI models from Google that can understand and create different types of things like words, pictures, and sounds all together.

Hallucination - When the AI makes up information that sounds real but isn't true. It's like when someone confidently gives an answer on a test but gets it completely wrong! Scientists are working hard to make AI hallucinate less often.

Inference - When the AI uses what it has learned to figure out an answer or create something new when you ask it a question, kind of like using what you learned in class to answer homework questions.

Instructions - The clear directions you give the AI, telling it exactly what you want it to do, like when you explain the rules of a game to a friend.

Iterative prompting - Trying again and again with different questions until you get the answer you want from the AI. Like playing "Hot and Cold," where you keep giving hints until someone finds the hidden object.

Large Language Model (LLM) - A super big AI program that has read tons and tons of books, websites, and articles, so it's really good at understanding and writing like a human. Examples include ChatGPT, Claude, and Gemini.

Learning - When a computer gets better at tasks by practicing with examples or following instructions, just like how you get better at things when you practice.

Machine learning - Teaching computers to learn on their own from examples instead of telling them exactly what to do for every single situation. Like how you learn to recognize dogs after seeing many different dogs.

<u>Model</u> - The trained computer program itself. Think of it as the AI's brain that has learned how to do certain jobs through practice.

<u>Multimodal AI</u> - AI that can understand different types of information at once, like both pictures AND words. Like how you can understand a comic book with both drawings and text.

<u>Natural Language Generation (NLG)</u> - How computers create text that sounds like a person wrote it, like an AI writing you a birthday card message that sounds like it came from a friend.

<u>Natural Language Processing (NLP)</u> - Helping computers understand human languages so they can read and make sense of what we write and say.

<u>Natural Language Understanding (NLU)</u> - How computers figure out what you really mean when you say something. Like understanding that "I'm dying" might just mean you're laughing really hard!

<u>Neural network</u> - A computer system built a bit like a human brain, with lots of connections that help it learn patterns. Kind of like how all the students in a classroom connect ideas by talking to each other.

<u>Output</u> - What the AI gives you back after you ask it something. It's the answer, story, picture, or whatever it created for you.

<u>Parameter</u> - These are like the AI's memory notes that it writes while learning. The more notes it can take, the smarter it usually gets! Modern LLMs have billions or even trillions of these notes.

<u>Pattern recognition</u> - The AI's ability to notice things that repeat or look similar. Like how you can spot stripes or polka dots on different clothes.

<u>Perplexity</u> - A score that shows how well an AI understands language. For example, when you're reading a book, if you understand it well, you're not surprised by what comes next.

<u>Prediction</u> - When the AI tries to guess what will happen next based on patterns it has seen before. Like how you might predict the end of a story.

<u>Pre-training</u> - The first step where an AI reads tons of books, websites, and articles to learn about the world before it learns to do specific tasks. Like going to elementary school before learning a specific sport or instrument.

<u>Prompt</u> - The message or question you send to the AI to make it do something. It's how you tell the AI what you want, like telling a waiter your food order.

<u>Prompt engineering</u> - The skill of writing really good questions to get the best answers from AI. It's like knowing exactly how to ask for directions so you don't get lost.

<u>RAG (Retrieval-Augmented Generation)</u> - A way to make AI smarter by letting it look up facts in a trusted information library before answering your question. Like how you might check a dictionary or encyclopedia when writing a school report.

<u>Reinforcement Learning (RL)</u> - Teaching a computer by giving it rewards when it does something good, like giving a dog a treat when it learns a new trick.

Reinforcement Learning from Human Feedback (RLHF) - Using real people to tell the AI when its answers are good or bad, to help it learn to be more helpful. Like having a coach give you tips during practice. This is a key way modern LLMs like ChatGPT and Claude are trained!

Role-playing prompting - Asking the AI to pretend it's someone specific when it answers you. Like saying "Pretend you're a pirate" and then it talks like "Arrr, matey!"

Safety alignment - Making sure AI is designed to be helpful, harmless, and honest. It's like teaching a powerful helper to always be careful and follow good safety rules.

Specificity - How clear and exact your instructions are. The more specific you are, like "Draw a purple dragon with green spots," the better the AI can understand what you want.

Supervised learning - Teaching an AI using examples with correct answers, like showing it pictures of dogs labeled "dog" and cats labeled "cat," so it learns to tell them apart.

Text-to-image models - Special AI that can create pictures based on your descriptions. You type in "a purple elephant riding a bicycle" and it draws it for you! Examples include DALL-E, Midjourney, and Stable Diffusion.

Token - A small piece of text, like a word or part of a word. Think of tokens as the LEGO bricks that AI uses to build sentences.

Training - The whole process of teaching an AI to get smarter, like how you learn through all your years at school.

Transfer learning - When an AI uses what it learned from one job to help with a new job. Like how learning to ride a bike helps you learn to ride a scooter more quickly.

Transformer - A special design for AI brains that's really good at understanding how words in a sentence connect to each other, even if they're far apart.

Unsupervised learning - Letting the AI figure out patterns all by itself without being told the right answers. Like giving you a box of toys and watching how you sort them without instructions.

User intent - What you really want the AI to understand or do, even if you don't explain it perfectly. Like when your parent knows you want a snack, even if you just say "I'm hungry."

Validation - Checking if the AI's work is correct and good enough. Like having someone check your homework before you turn it in.

Weights - Special numbers inside the AI's brain that show which connections are important. The AI adjusts these numbers as it learns, like how you might decide which facts are most important when studying.

Zero-shot prompting - Asking the AI to do something new that it hasn't seen an example of before. Like asking you to draw an animal you've never drawn before, using what you know about drawing other animals.

AI Quiz

1. What are Large Language Models (LLMs)?
   a) Robots that can talk
   b) A type of AI trained on text that can understand and generate human language
   c) Special keyboards for typing faster
   d) Machines that translate between different languages

2. How do scientists create Large Language Models?
   a) By building robot bodies for them
   b) By feeding them enormous amounts of text
   c) By teaching them one word at a time
   d) By connecting them to the internet

3. When LLMs create text, what are they actually doing?
   a) Copying from books they've read
   b) Making smart guesses about what words should come next
   c) Understanding the meaning of every word
   d) Asking humans for help

4. What do we call the instructions we give to language models?
   a) Commands
   b) Orders
   c) Prompts
   d) Directions

5. What is prompt engineering?
   a) Building physical prompts for theater actors
   b) The skill of writing clear instructions for AI
   c) Creating new AI models
   d) Programming computers

6. In the coffee shop drink analogy, what does a very specific drink order represent?

a) A poorly written prompt

b) An AI that doesn't understand

c) A well-written, detailed prompt

d) A confused barista

7. Which of these is a good prompt engineering technique?

a) Using as few words as possible

b) Being vague so the AI can be creative

c) Providing examples of what you want

d) Using difficult vocabulary to test the AI

8. What does "iterative prompting" mean?

a) Asking the same question repeatedly

b) Changing your prompt based on previous responses

c) Giving the AI multiple questions at once

d) Writing very long prompts

9. Why should you NOT ask an AI to write your entire homework assignment?

a) It would take too long

b) AI can't write well enough

c) It wouldn't help you learn

d) The AI might get tired

10. What's a responsible way to use AI for schoolwork?

a) Having it write everything for you

b) Asking it to create practice questions to test your knowledge

c) Letting it decide what you should study

d) Skipping homework entirely

11. What information should you NEVER share with AI tools?

    a) Your favorite color

    b) Your home address

    c) Questions about homework

    d) Your favorite book

12. What do Large Language Models learn from when they're being created?

    a) Watching human conversations

    b) Playing video games

    c) Text from books, websites, and articles

    d) Taking online courses

13. What's the main difference between how LLMs and humans understand language?

    a) LLMs read faster than humans

    b) Humans need more practice

    c) LLMs recognize patterns but don't have real-world experiences

    d) Humans can only learn one language at a time

14. Which is an example of providing context in a prompt?

    a) "Write a story."

    b) "Write anything you want."

    c) "Write a story about dragons."

    d) "We are planning a surprise party for my Granny's eightieth birthday. What kinds of games were popular when she was my age?"

15. What's a good way to make an LLM's response more specific?

    a) Use fewer words in your prompt

    b) Tell it exactly what you want included

    c) Type in all capital letters

    d) Wait longer for a response

16. How is AI's relationship with human jobs described in the book?
    a) AI will completely replace all human jobs
    b) AI works best when partnering with humans
    c) AI cannot do any human jobs
    d) AI will only work in factories

17. What's compared to AI's impact on jobs?
    a) The invention of cars
    b) The invention of electricity
    c) The invention of personal computers
    d) The invention of smartphones

18. How are LLMs described when they write about experiences they've never had?
    a) They're lying about experiences
    b) They know what words go together but don't have real experiences
    c) They're repeating what someone told them
    d) They're making random guesses

19. What technique is being used when you ask an LLM to pretend it's a firefighter?
    a) Iterative prompting
    b) Role-playing prompting
    c) Example prompting
    d) Breaking tasks down

20. What does the book compare LLMs building stories to?
    a) Painting a picture
    b) Baking a cake
    c) Solving a math problem
    d) Fitting pieces together like a giant puzzle made of words

21. Large Language Models are also known as _____.

22. LLMs don't truly understand like people do because they don't have _____ like we do.

23. When you give LLMs text, they guess what comes next, one _____ at a time.

24. The special skill of writing really good instructions for AI is called _____.

25. When ordering a drink, asking for "a drink" could get you anything, but asking for a detailed order is like giving an AI a _____ prompt.

26. Providing _____ of what you want helps the AI understand better.

27. When writing prompts, it helps to include what kind of _____ you need.

28. Asking the AI to think about the best way to answer before starting makes the LLM think more _____ about your prompt.

29. Having a conversation with the AI where you give it feedback is called _____ prompting.

30. AI assistants are meant to help us learn and be more creative, not to do our _____ for us.

31. Using a calculator for math is compared to using _____ as a tool.

32. When using AI tools. we should never share personal details like our home
_____.

33. In the future. AI will work best when it _____ with humans.

34. Learning to talk to AI properly isn't just about homework help. but preparing
for when these tools will be part of many different types of _____.

35. AI isn't magical or scary—it's a _____. like any other technology.

36. The "C" in the C.R.A.F.T. method stands for _____. which means giving AI
background information about your work.

37. When AI writes about ice cream without ever having tasted it. this shows
that LLMs don't have _____ like humans do.

38. Sometimes AI might give an unfair or one-sided answer because it learned
from things people wrote. which can be _____.

39. The "F" in the C.R.A.F.T. method tells the AI how to _____ the answer.
such as making a list or organizing information with chapters.

40. AI that can understand both pictures AND words is called _____ AI.
similar to how you can understand a comic book with both drawings and text.

41. Large Language Models are actually robots.

42. LLMs have read almost every book ever written.

43. LLMs understand words the same way humans do.

44. The more information LLMs study, the better they get at recognizing human language patterns.

45. When using an LLM, it's better to be vague so it can be creative.

46. You can tell an LLM what you don't want to see in its answer.

47. Your first prompt will always get you exactly what you need.

48. AI assistants sometimes make mistakes.

49. It's a good idea to ask an AI to write your entire homework assignment.

50. You can ask an AI to check your work after you've done it yourself.

51. AI systems might share your personal information with others.

52. Learning prompt engineering now will be valuable for the future.

53. AI works best when it replaces humans completely.

54. Asking an AI for practice questions can help you study better.

55. AI is just a tool, and how useful it is depends on how well you use it.

Quiz Answers

Multiple Choice	Fill in the Blank	True/False
1. b	21. LLMs	41. False
2. b	22. experiences	42. True
3. b	23. word	43. False
4. c	24. prompt engineering	44. True
5. b	25. specific	45. False
6. c	26. examples	46. True
7. c	27. information	47. False
8. b	28. deeply	48. True
9. c	29. iterative	49. False
10. b	30. thinking	50. True
11. b	31. AI	51. True
12. c	32. address	52. True
13. c	33. partners	53. False
14. d	34. jobs	54. True
15. b	35. tool	55. True
16. b	36. context	
17. c	37. senses	
18. b	38. biased	
19. b	39. format	
20. d	40. multimodal	

Prompting Exercises

In the following activities, you'll see how giving more details in your prompt helps an AI understand precisely what you want. Try each prompt separately, and see how the response changes!

Assignment 1

Write a paragraph about African elephants.

Prompt #1: Tell me about African elephants.

Prompt #2: Write a paragraph describing what African elephants look like and where they live.

Prompt #3: Write an informative paragraph about African elephants that explains their physical features, habitat, and one interesting fact about their social behavior. Use language that a 10-year-old would understand.

Prompt #4: Write an engaging paragraph about African elephants for 3rd-grade children. Include details about how they differ from Asian elephants, describe their natural habitat in the African savanna, mention their endangered status, and explain at least one way how elephant families care for each other. Use vivid language and keep the vocabulary appropriate for 10-year-olds.

Assignment 2

Write a poem about the ocean.

Prompt #1: Write a poem about the ocean.

Prompt #2: Write a short poem about the ocean that includes the sounds of waves and seagulls.

Prompt #3: Write a four-line poem about the ocean that uses rhyming couplets. Include imagery about the sunset reflecting on the water and how it makes you feel peaceful.

Prompt #4: Write a haiku poem about the ocean at sunset for elementary school children. Use simple words that evoke the colors (deep blue, orange, gold), sounds (gentle waves), and feelings (calm, wonder) of being at the beach in the evening. Make sure it follows the traditional 5-7-5 syllable pattern of haiku.

Assignment 3

Create an image of a dinosaur.

Prompt #1: Draw a dinosaur.

Prompt #2: Create an image of a T-Rex dinosaur in a forest.

Prompt #3: Generate a friendly cartoon image of a green T-Rex dinosaur playing with butterflies in a prehistoric jungle with volcanoes in the background. Make it suitable for a children's book.

Prompt #4: Create a detailed digital illustration of a baby Tyrannosaurus Rex with big expressive eyes. The dinosaur should be lime green with tiny purple spots and sitting in a lush prehistoric jungle. Include colorful butterflies flying around its head. In the far background, add a smoking volcano and pterodactyls flying in a clear blue sky. The style should be cute and non-scary, appropriate for a 8-year-old's bedroom wall, with bright colors.

Assignment 4

Create a cookie recipe.

Prompt #1: Give me a cookie recipe.

Prompt #2: Write a recipe for chocolate chip cookies that is easy to make.

Prompt #3: Create a simple chocolate chip cookie recipe for kids to make with adult supervision. Include ingredients, measurements, step-by-step instructions, and baking temperature and time.

Prompt #4: Design a fun, kid-friendly chocolate chip cookie recipe that 8-10 year olds can make. Include a list of ingredients with exact measurements (using cups and teaspoons), all required kitchen tools, prep time, cooking time, and temperature (in both Fahrenheit and Celsius). Provide numbered steps with clear instructions, highlighting where adult help is needed (like using the oven). Add safety tips, suggestions for cookie variations (like adding sprinkles), and a note about how to tell when the cookies are perfectly done.

Home or Classroom Project Ideas

AI Experience Journal

Keep a journal for a week of all the AI you encounter or use. At the end of the week, discuss: Were you surprised by how much or how little AI you used? How did the AI help? Were there any problems?

AI Ethics Committee

Form a "ethics committee" to create guidelines for responsible AI use in your home or school. Consider questions like: When is it appropriate to use AI for homework? How should we give credit when AI helps us create something?

Future Vision Board

Create a vision board (digital or physical) showing ways AI might be part of your life in 10 years. Include both exciting possibilities and potential concerns.

Compare and Contrast

Try the same prompt on different AI tools if available (like different chatbots or image generators). How are the responses different? Which do you prefer and why?

Take a look at other subjects Lila and Andy are learning about...

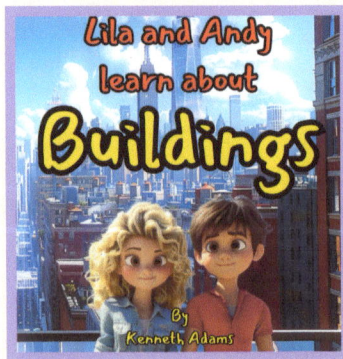

Lila and Andy learn about **Buildings**
By Kenneth Adams

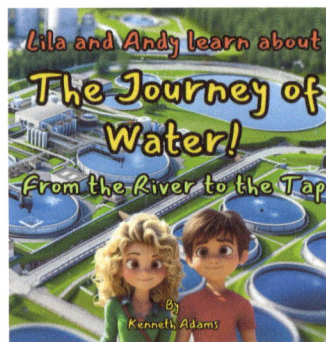

Lila and Andy learn about **The Journey of Water!** From the River to the Tap
By Kenneth Adams

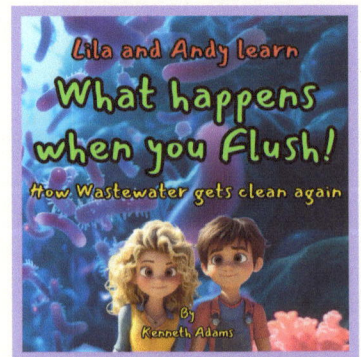

Lila and Andy learn **What happens when you Flush!** How Wastewater gets clean again
By Kenneth Adams

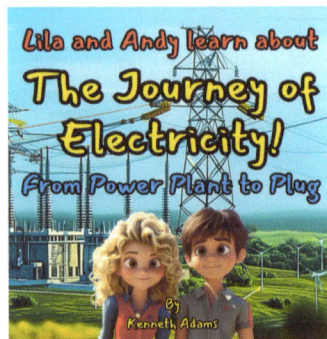

Lila and Andy learn about **The Journey of Electricity!** From Power Plant to Plug
By Kenneth Adams

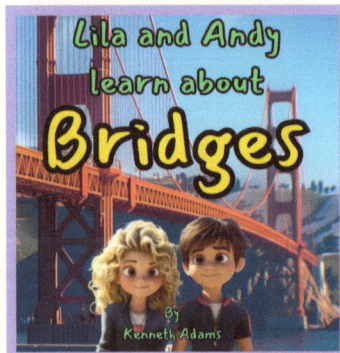

Lila and Andy learn about **Bridges**
By Kenneth Adams

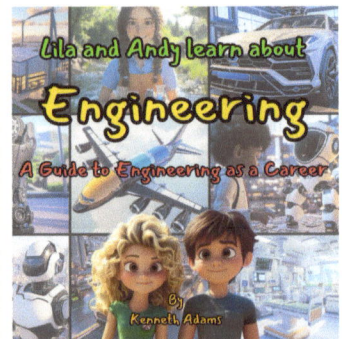

Lila and Andy learn about **Engineering** A Guide to Engineering as a Career
By Kenneth Adams

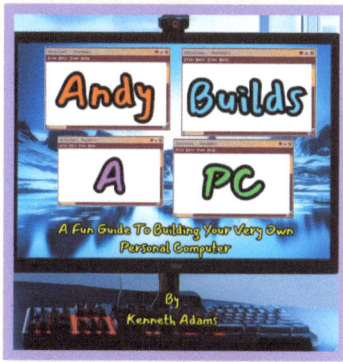

Andy Builds A PC

A Fun Guide To Building Your Very Own Personal Computer

By Kenneth Adams

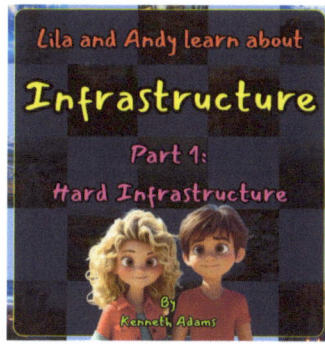

Lila and Andy learn about Infrastructure

Part 1: Hard Infrastructure

By Kenneth Adams

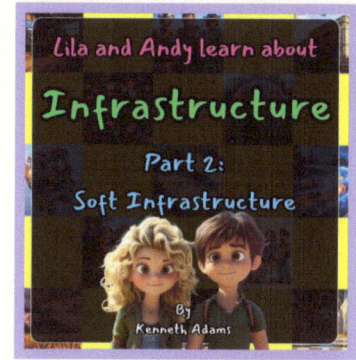

Lila and Andy learn about Infrastructure

Part 2: Soft Infrastructure

By Kenneth Adams

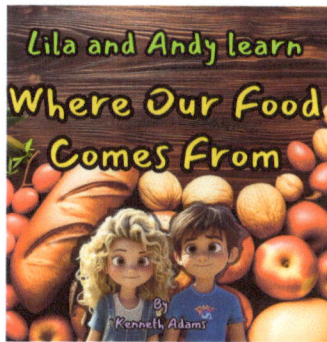

Lila and Andy learn Where Our Food Comes From

By Kenneth Adams

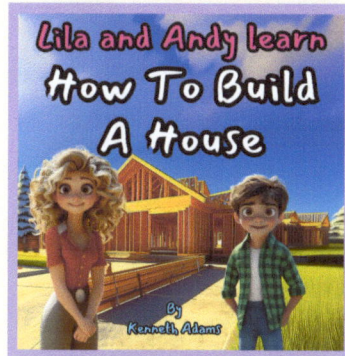

Lila and Andy learn How To Build A House

By Kenneth Adams

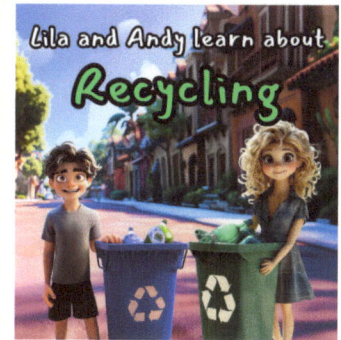

Lila and Andy learn about Recycling

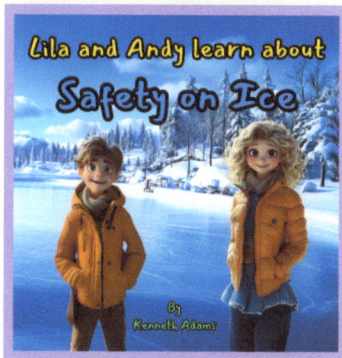

Lila and Andy learn about Safety on Ice

By Kenneth Adams

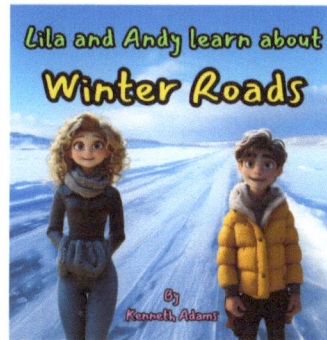

Lila and Andy learn about Winter Roads

By Kenneth Adams

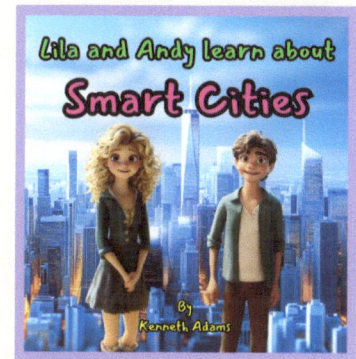

Lila and Andy learn about Smart Cities

By Kenneth Adams

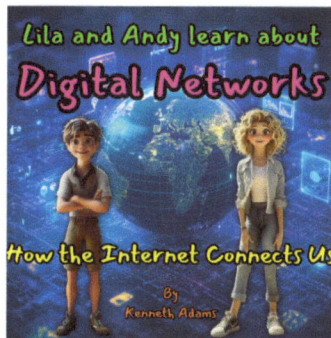

Lila and Andy learn about Digital Networks

How the Internet Connects Us

By Kenneth Adams

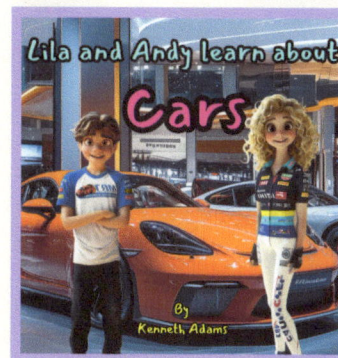

Lila and Andy learn about Cars

By Kenneth Adams